Il Diario di Kaspar Hauser
The Diary of Kaspar Hauser

in memory of Lucio Mariani

PAOLO FEBBRARO

THE DIARY OF KASPAR HAUSER

translated from the Italian
by Anthony Molino

Negative Capability
PRESS

The Diary of Kaspar Hauser

© 2017, Paolo Febbraro
Translated from the Italian by Anthony Molino

Cover and Interior Design by Megan Cary
Cover Artwork by Oliana Spazzoli

ISBN: 978-0-9986777-0-5
Library of Congress Control Number: 2017902293

Negative Capability Press
62 Ridgelawn Drive East
Mobile, Alabama 36608
United States of America
www.negativecapabilitypress.org
facebook.com/negativecapabilitypress

Ci sono imbecilli superficiali e imbecilli profondi.
K. KRAUS

There are superficial imbeciles and there are
profound imbeciles.
K. KRAUS

A REQUISITE PREAMBLE

*The writings here rendered in Italian were found in a small farming
area near Regensburg, in Bavaria, among the papers of Herr Franz Paul
Webern, upon the latter's death in 1830.*

*It was Webern's nephew Friedrich who, amid copies of letters, notes
concerning the household budget, and two signed copies of his uncle's
testament, chanced upon a folder on which was written "The Diary of
Kaspar Hauser". The handwriting that marked the pages therein, as well
as the latter's content, were found to differ significantly from all the other
documents, leading the young man to seek out explanations from each
and every relative of the deceased. Thus from the stories collected emerged
the figure of said Kaspar Hauser, a young man who had resided with the
Webern family in the years between 1811 to 1815, when he died tragically
in an ambush.*

*Many years later, Friedrich Webern compiled a first edition of these
writings, published in Regensburg in March 1875 in a print run of three
hundred copies. In his preface, the elderly Webern affirmed that he'd never
heard any mention on the part of his uncle concerning the presence, or
even the existence, of anyone by the name of Kaspar Hauser. That edition
serves as the direct source for these translations, with regards to both the
texts themselves and the order in which they hereby appear. No trace was
ever found, instead, of the original manuscript: not even among the papers
which, at the death of Friedrich Webern in 1883, were on display at the
University of ***, where they were archived only to be destroyed in 1944.*

The information available to us concerning the Diary's *author is therefore
limited to the preface penned by Webern for the volume he himself had
edited, which I offer here in my translation.*

Kaspar Hauser was found on 21 April 1811, at dawn, in
the main square of the village of Eisen, near Regensburg.
He was standing straight, resting his back against a tree. It
was in this position that he was discovered by the saddler
Grimmel, who was about to open his shop. In short, after

the burghermaster and commanding officer of the local garrison were summoned, it was verified that the individual in question – between thirty and forty years of age, of below-average height, sporting pitch-black hair and eyes – was altogether incapable of articulating meaningful words, or even of expressing himself with intelligible signs and gestures. He wore ordinary clothes, albeit too tight for his build, and no shoes. Lacking a letter of presentation or travel papers of any sort, he was housed in a cell of the garrison and assigned to the tutelage of the burghermaster Hauser. While efforts were undertaken to gather information and ascertain the provenance of the man, a physician, dr. Paul Feyerand, was summoned from the nearest town and declared him unfit for walking and talking, and unable to recognize and use even the most basic of everyday objects.

Research into the subject's past, which proved superficial at best, yielded no results. Meanwhile, the townsfolk who'd gather by the door to the cell where the foundling was harbored made him the object of curiosity, ridicule, and far-reaching conjecture. The man did prove able, ultimately, of feeding himself, even though he ignored the correct use of knife-and-fork. His precautionary detention came to an end when the head of the Webern family, my uncle Franz Paul, requested and was granted custody of the foundling, who by then had come to be known as Hauser and upon whom the name Kaspar had been bestowed. My uncle, a most charitable man with a good heart, took Kaspar home with him, to his country estate, situated at a remove of three miles from Eisen.

From then on, and for four years, the man named Kaspar Hauser was educated with love and understanding by my uncle and his family. He learned to walk, to eat properly and to express himself in simple but correct German. All the same, he remained an obscure and solitary figure, as meek and submissive as, on occasion, he could prove reluctant to embrace even the simplest of common-sense teachings. My aunt Hanna, for example, relates that he was a good student of arithmetic, but disdained the study of grammar. Only once was a tutor summoned, but the gentleman left after but an hour, exceedingly irritated and intent on never returning again. All this, probably, because Kaspar Hauser was not at the level of a normal student. He would apply himself to the study of the most basic elements of every subject matter with a passion that was painful to behold. And if he detested the study of grammar this was no indication of an aversion of his, borne of indolence or ineptitude; to the contrary, he would make absurdly strenuous efforts to refute its classifications.

Ultimately, it proved impossible to proceed beyond a level of elementary instruction. Kaspar did betray a certain musical talent, but was totally inept in understanding the fundamental concepts of Theology, Philosophy and Law. Moreover, no one could tell me with any degree of precision whether Kaspar had assimilated the Christian faith. On one hand he showed no inclination to frequent the Church, but personally I do not believe this to be a decisive factor. On the other, my uncle Franz Paul made sure to provide him with ample opportunity for devotional readings. Indeed, it seems that Kaspar never read novels. There was one time, however, towards the end of his life, when he was seen holding a small book authored by a minor poet of the early 18th century. On that occasion, word has it that he could be heard repeatedly exclaiming these very words: "Now I hear the voice!"

The preceding paragraphs comprise all we know, and will ever know, about Kaspar Hauser. The note by Friedrich Webern continues, in fact, with a portrayal of various family members, primarily of those who had direct knowledge of the foundling. This, in an obvious attempt to garner as many second-hand accounts as possible to substantiate the story. Webern then proceeds to focus the attention of scholars on the sociological, and even the medical-diagnostic, insights afforded by the writings contained in the Diary. Some years later, these supposed insights inspired two psychiatrists from Heidelberg, Peter Himmer and Karl-Heinz Göbel, to adopt some of the expressions for the appendix to an 1889 treatise of theirs entitled Forms and figures of mental retardation. A study of idiocy. The volume, published in Heidelberg by the local University, included a dozen or so of the original texts, which were supplemented by ponderous notes of a highly specialized nature.

From a textual standpoint, the original manuscript discovered by Friedrich Webern — according to observations recorded in his note of 1875 — revealed nothing out of the ordinary. The title on the folder in which the sheets of the "Diary" were preserved was penned by the hand of Franz Paul Webern; the handwriting of the individual texts (one and only one per page), was "neat, almost elegant, surely the result of concentrated effort and not of haphazard scrawling"; the ink was of the kind commonly in use at the time, while the paper matched that typically employed by the elderly Webern for his own note-taking. None of the texts was dated, nor could a plausible date be attributed to any of them; the individual sheets of paper were neither numbered nor signed.

What remains to be justified, if at all possible, is the appearance of this belated Italian version. What value may inhere — at a time when the heyday of philosophy is long behind us and technology has triumphed as the paramount form of human activity — in the words of an odd man, who lived in the Bavarian countryside in the early 1800's, likely afflicted by a serious mental disorder, whose personality was forged in the span of but a few years and barred, moreover, to any scrutiny? The reader is owed a reply: a reply that can only prove to be a concise attempt at interpretation.

It's very probable that, from the depths of a childhood congealed in its mental state, which likely persisted due to the erasure of a prolonged and mysterious trauma, Kaspar Hauser proved able to communicate the absurdity of his life and times thanks to the very language he so mistrusted — an attitude which the reader will verify time and again throughout these pages. The "idiot child", a figure which enjoys a tradition of its own in diverse literatures, was to find in Kaspar a quasi-paradigmatic incarnation: only to end up, initially, in a book by two positivist psychiatrists before disappearing again, in the fogs of a near-impenetrable enigma.

It is a well-known fact that one of our most acclaimed poets identifies "the little child" inhabiting his soul as the most genuine source of all poetry.* Along these lines the views he put forth one-hundred years ago are still largely shared. The shortcoming in his argument, however, is that children are usually not well-versed in the study of botany or ornithology: thus making for a misunderstanding of a theoretical nature, notwithstanding its poetic seductiveness. In the compositions that follow, configured as poems on the page, we are perhaps confronted by the unique opportunity to experience the fruits of an authentic childhood — made possible, paradoxically, by the thirty, thirty-five or forty years of Kaspar Hauser. An alien solitude is at the root of his communications, which reflect the gargantuan effort of naming the world for the first time. Indeed, it's as if his thoughts genuinely betray the first-ever attempt to extract sense from the world. One is left with the strong and mysterious sensation that this first attempt is already a fully mature one: as absolute as it is relative, albeit soaked in the simplicity of the senses. Kaspar appears to us as a sort of etymology of the human. Etymology, in fact, studies the root of meaning, the denotation or initial impression; it is the original of a copy, the name in itself, the authentic. And like everything authentic, the etymon is stripped of the layers of errors and bad habits; of the transpiration of other words, other places, other moments; of that mobile crust of "what really got said" that sediments upon every word we use. It is stripped of common sense, of every sense that is vulgar, impure, illegitimate and piously (or pitifully) necessary. Such is Kaspar Hauser the man. And so does the chasm between such an interpretation and that offered by the positivism of Himmer and Göbel provide the measure of the painful awareness that the XX century has impressed and continues to impress on us all. This, perhaps, is the meaning of the defenseless absurdities of Kaspar Hauser, the value of his indefensible confutations of what is, or perhaps was, common knowledge.

*Translator's note: The reference is to the Italian poet Giovanni Pascoli (1855-1912) and his celebrated essay *Il fanciullino* ("The Little Child"), wherein the author claims that in every man there persists an eternal child, awash in wonder and poetry.

THE DIARY OF KASPAR HAUSER

Il freddo.

Mi divincolo
alzo le braccia
ma ugualmente la maglia
s'infila e scende ai fianchi,
si prende le ascelle.
Uscendo mi accorgo
che aveva ragione.

The cold.

I wriggle
lift my arms
all the same my sweater
slips on, down my hips
wraps my armpits.
I go out, realize
it was right.

"È una mela, Kaspar.
L'albero che vedi la produce
dal cuore della terra
così che noi possiamo nutrircene
quando ogni altra pianta dorme.
Così è stato provveduto.
Dietro alle cose, c'è la verità".

Alzo la mano e non arrivo.
Ed è grande e rossa.
Un'altra è morta marrone in terra.
Qualcos'altro la mangia.
Dietro la verità, le cose.

"It's an apple, Kaspar.
The tree you see yields it
from the heart of the earth
for it to nourish us
when every other plant sleeps.
So has been decreed.
Behind all things, is truth."

I try reaching with my hand and can't.
And it is big and red.
Another died brown on the ground.
Something else eats it.
Behind the truth, all things.

Il contadino appena dopo
la pioggia a metà luglio
ringrazia il cielo.[1]

[1] *Quest'ultimo "verso" suona:* **dankt dem Himmelszelt**, *ovvero,*
letteralmente: rende grazie alla tenda del cielo.

The peasant right after
the mid-July rain
gives thanks to the sky. [1]

[1] The original German reads *dankt dem Himmelszelt:* literally,
"gives thanks to the tent in the sky."

Accanto alla finestra
guardo in giardino.
Poi passo la porta.
Ora, se guardo, ho il giardino
alle spalle ma il mio posto
è sparito.

From the window
I look out at the garden.
Then I pass by the door.
Now, if I look, the garden
is behind me but my place
has disappeared.

"Siamo noi a vederle piccole, Kaspar.
In realtà sono enormi,
la loro luce è fioca
solo per la distanza".

"Quanto sei alto, Franz?"
"Un metro e settanta".
Poi corro forte e lo stringo
vicinissimo.
"Ora quanto?"

"It's that we see them small, Kaspar.
Actually, they're huge,
their light is feeble
only because of the distance."

"How tall are you, Franz?"
"Five foot eight."
Then I run fast and hug him
real close.
"And now?"

"No, Franz.
No, No, No, No".

Poi apro gli occhi
e lui è vivo.

"No, Franz.
No, No, No, No."

Then I open my eyes
and he is alive.

"Ca-val-lo, Kaspar".

Ma impara i nomi degli animali
dopo che hai visto due di essi almeno.

"Horse, Kaspar. Horse."

But learn the names of animals
after you've seen at least two of each.

La neve è bianca.

La notte è nera.

La nebbia, al mattino,
mescola.

Snow is white.

Night is black.

The morning fog
mixes things.

"No, Kaspar.
Sotto la neve
l'albero è sempre verde.
Vedrai in primavera".

Invece d'inverno
l'albero è completamente
nero.

"No, Kaspar.
Beneath the snow
the tree is always green.
You'll see in spring."

In winter instead
the tree is completely
black.

"Vieni a passeggiare, Franz?"
"Più tardi, Kaspar, sto leggendo".

Chiedere se leggere
è più di passeggiare.

"Will you stroll with me, Franz?"
"Later, Kaspar, I'm reading."

Ask if reading
is more than strolling.

Dopo la pioggia cammino
e il fango delle orme
mi segue in silenzio.
Su roccia torno solo.

After the rain I walk
and the mud of footprints
follows me in silence.
On rock I return alone.

"Guarda, Kaspar.
Il lago, e in quel punto
il ruscello".

La pianura perde
la sua pazienza.

"Look, Kaspar.
The lake, and there
the stream."

The plain loses
its patience.

"La terra pende, Kaspar.
E il ruscello, vedi, scende a valle.
Per la pendenza l'acqua
continuamente corre".

Pure, il rumore è immobile.

"The earth bends, Kaspar.
And the stream, see, slopes to the valley.
Because of the bend the water
runs on and on."

Yet, the sound stands still.

Vado insieme al ruscello
lui rallenta la corsa.
Salgo a vedergli la fonte
l'acqua si arrabbia veloce.

I run with the stream
he slows down.
I climb to see his source
the water gets angry fast.

"Ascoltare con gli occhi:
ecco il miracolo della lettura.
Quando non puoi avvertire la voce
lo scritto ti giunge ugualmente.
Imparerai, Kaspar".
"Ma parlami ancora, Franz".

"To listen with one's eyes:
such is the miracle of reading.
When you can't sense the voice
what's written still reaches you.
You'll learn, Kaspar."
"But Franz, talk to me more."

Apro il libro poco.
Poso gli occhi dentro.
Lo chiudo.
(Non bisbigliano).

I open the book a little.
And rest my eyes inside.
I close it.
(They don't whisper.)

*I nomi è come
la pioggia nel ruscello.*

The names is like
rain in the stream.

"Certo che usa la grammatica!
Ogni poeta, Kaspar,
è un maestro della lingua".

Lì tuttavia le parole
spostano.

"Of course he uses grammar!
Every poet, Kaspar,
is a master of language."

But there words
displace.

Faccio leggere a Franz.
Sorride e mi parla.

La scrittura è la stessa
ma i pensieri tornano sotto.

I let Franz read.
He smiles and talks to me.

The writing is the same
but the thoughts go back under.

"Se ieri hai mangiato sei pere
e oggi altre cinque,
quante pere hai mangiato in tutto?".
"Cinque".

"If yesterday you ate six pears
and today another five,
how many pears have you eaten altogether?"
"Five."

"Era l'uomo, Kaspar,
che trainava il carro,
non il contrario!"
"No, Franz. Ora infatti
l'uomo cammina ancora,
il carro è stanco fermo
a riposare".

"It was the man, Kaspar,
who pulled the cart,
not the opposite!"
"No, Franz. In fact now
the man is still walking,
the cart is tired, stopped
to rest."

"La carrozza parte alle undici
da Piazza Königsberg. Fa' in fretta".
Un nome allo spazio
un numero al tempo
e grande memoria.

"The coach leaves at eleven
from Königsberg Square. Hurry up."
A name for space
a number for time
and a big memory.

Se alle undici la carrozza parte
cosa rimane della città?
Controllare.

If the coach leaves at eleven
what's left of the city?
Be sure to check.

Muri e pareti.
Molte facciate.
La città è se la campagna
viene circondata.

Walls and partitions.
So many facades.
The city is if the country
gets surrounded.

Bambini hanno giocato fino a sera.
Franz è nel letto.
Finché uno è giovane
è sempre giovane.
Quando è vecchio
non molto è vecchio.

Children played till evening.
Franz is in bed.
As long as one is young
he's young always.
When he's old
not much old.

"Futuro è ciò che hai davanti.
Passato, dietro".
Io mi volto.

"Ho capito, Kaspar. Allora
futuro è ciò che è fuori.
Passato, dentro".

Il tempo entra?

"Future is what's before you.
Past, behind you."
I look back.

"I understand, Kaspar. Then
future is what's outside.
Past, inside."

Does time enter?

"No, Kaspar. Dio è buono".
"Come il pane caldo?"
"Più ancora".
"Come le fragole, allora".
"Ma egli è eterno".

(Troppe fragole)

"No, Kaspar. God is good."
"Like fresh-baked bread?"
"Even more."
"Like strawberries, then."
"But he is eternal."

(Too many strawberries)

"Rientra, Kaspar.
C'è vento".
"Vedo, Franz, i rami
spingono aria".

"Come back inside, Kaspar.
It's windy."
"I can see, Franz, the branches
push the air."

Al vento sbattono le porte.
Ogni stanza vuole tenersi
i suoi pensieri.

In the wind doors slam.
Every room wants to keep
its thoughts.

Picchio la mano sul tavolo.
Succede il rumore.
Di fuori i bambini sono colpiti
dalla meraviglia.

I bang my hand on the table.
Noise happens.
Children outside get struck
with wonder.

Le parole tappano i buchi
degli oggetti.
Di notte le cose
riprendono fiato.

Words plug the holes
of objects.
At night things
catch their breath.

"Apri la finestra, Kaspar".
"No, Franz. Voglio rimanere".

"Open the window, Kaspar."
"No, Franz. I want to stay."

Dove sono i luoghi, Franz?
"Fuori".
Dove sono i nomi?
"Dentro".
E il tavolo della cucina?
"È fuori".
E perché fra i campi so
che in cucina c'è un tavolo?
"È il ricordo, Kaspar".
E se i luoghi sono fuori
e il ricordo dentro
io sono in mezzo?

Where are the places, Franz?
"Outside."
Where are the names?
"Inside."
And the kitchen table?
"It's outside."
Then how do I know when I'm in the fields
that in the kitchen there's a table?
"It's the memory, Kaspar."
And if the places are outside
and the memory inside
am I in the middle?

"Entra anche tu, Kaspar:
è solo un vecchio amico".
"Non ci entro, Franz.
Questa casa
è molto superficiale".

"You too, Kaspar, come in,
he's only an old friend."
"I will not enter, Franz.
This house
is very superficial."

In sogno ci sono tre uomini
e sono davanti a una parete.
Uno dice: vado dove scrive la mano.
L'altro dice: vado dove pulsa il cuore.
Il terzo deve andare di qua o di là.
Invece si mette a scavare.
Scava finché trova una pietra dura.
La pietra dice: di qua o di là.
La vanga stanca dice: di qua o di là.
Il piede malfermo: di qua o di là.
L'uomo vorrebbe rompere la pietra
gettare la vanga
rinunciare al piede.

In a dream there are three men
and they're before a wall.
One says: I go where the hand writes.
The other says: I go where the heart beats.
The third must go here or there.
Instead he starts to dig.
He digs until he hits a stone.
The stone says: here or there.
The tired spade says: here or there.
The wobbly foot says: here or there.
The man would like to break the stone
throw away the spade
forsake the foot.

*"Era un sogno, Kaspar,
non la realtà".*

Facevo finta?

"It was a dream, Kaspar,
not reality."

Was I pretending?

"La Natura, Kaspar".
Io allora misuro i passi
fra un albero e l'altro.
Non nascere è un modo di morire?
In mezzo c'è spazio e nient'altro.
Non vedo Natura
ma due alberi lontani
di quasi undici passi.

"Nature, Kaspar."
I then count the steps
between one tree and the next.
Is not being born a way to die?
In the middle is space and no more.
I see no Nature
only two distant trees
nearly eleven steps apart.

Quello in su è il cateto.
Quello in basso è il cateto.
L'ipotenusa lo ha spezzato,
ma è più corta.

The top one is the cathetus.
The bottom one is the cathetus.
The hypothenuse snapped it,
but is shorter.

La sera scorda l'aspetto delle cose.
Io stringo duro il bicchiere.
Premo il letto.
La notte poi dimentica me.

Evening forgets the look of things.
I clutch the glass.
Press on the bed.
Then the night unknows me.

Nel sogno l'uomo sente le voci:
o di qua o di là.
Lui dice: resto,
il tempo mi farà liquido
da scendere nelle fessure
o minerale che taglia la pietra.
Stanchi e vecchi
compiuto il cerchio
i due viandanti
lo rivedono albero.

In the dream the man hears voices:
here or there.
He says: I will stay,
time will make me liquid
to seep into the cracks,
or mineral, that cuts stone.
Tired and old
now come full-circle
the two travelers see him
turned tree.

EPILOGUE

Kaspar Hauser's death was tragically senseless. In September 1815, startled while taking a walk by two armed bandits, he responded to their intimations by suddenly turning around and, upon closing his eyes, remaining motionless. The bandits became impatient when confronted by a refusal whose significance they couldn't fathom. Before escaping they struck him repeatedly with careless precision. The attending physician later said that the wound which proved fatal had nonetheless left him alive for a few minutes, suspended between the grass and his final, unredeemable thoughts.

Still today Kaspar's strange attitude in the face of extreme danger provides food for thought. It's difficult to understand if it was borne simply out of terror or of an instinctively philosophical stance. Possibly, since Kaspar registered as real only what he perceived, it sufficed to turn around and close his eyes to believe he'd erased the bandits. His immobility, however, does remain enigmatic.

One is led to think that the solution may be of a different order. Ultimately, the problem was always how to make the two killers disappear. The memory of them, in fact, compounded by the unbearable thought of Evil itself, would have continued to burn in his mind, and therefore in every fragment of his present. Where he is now, instead, it makes no difference to Kaspar whether he or his killers really disappeared.

No message, only a brutal fact. Perhaps this is the mystery of the death of Kaspar Hauser.

APPENDIX

Dear Febbraro,

Enclosed please find the copy of *The Diary of Kaspar Hauser*
you'd sent me some months ago. I'll say right off that your
misgivings regarding the precision — or the force — of
the translation seem excessive. As you will gather from
the text, alongside the lone error of little consequence
noted in the fifth "poem", I have suggested but two
changes — merely stylistic in nature — to the tenth and
the twenty-sixth. Suggestions which you in no way should
feel obliged to accept. As per the inordinate delay in
my reply, I will say that it is in no way ascrivable to prior
commitments or engagements involving travel or whatnot;
no, my tardiness has simply to do with a consideration of
a different order, an "exterior" one, if you will: namely,
that I do not believe your booklet is one that can demand
an editor's urgent attention. Still, while apologizing
sincerely, I can do no better than to justify myself with a
pretense as embarrassing and uncoventional as it is, shall I
say, intimate. Rarely, and I think you'll agree, are we cap-
tured or enthralled by works written by others which, via
some auroral signposts or intuitions, we haven't already
written ourselves. It is for this reason that what meets our
favor are only forms and thoughts that perpetuate, or
go so far as to complete, our own. Where completion is
concerned, few are the works capable of inflicting such
mortifying bliss: what is certain, however, is that your
Kaspar has retraced in me a pre-existing path which now
returns in plain view and offers me, as a result, the ease

— or perhaps the anxiety — to survey the luxuriant vegetation of a forest abounding with impressions and ideas.

But allow me to come to the point. I am sure you are familiar with Mikhail Bakhtin's essay "Forms of Time and the Chronotope in the Novel," published in his book *The Dialogic Imagination.*[1] In that essay Bakhtin talks at a certain point about the "functions of the Rogue, Clown and Fool." These figures, known not only to Western literature, are ancient: "If one were to drop a historical sounding-lead into these artistic images, it would not touch bottom in any of them — they are that deep." So says Bakhtin in the English translation of his essay. You will recall, I trust, that the rogue, the clown and the fool "create around themselves their own special little world", where they all enjoy "a distinctive feature that is as well a privilege — the right to be *other* in this world, the right not to make common cause with any single one of the existing categories that life makes available; none of these categories quite suits them, they see the underside and the falseness of every situation." It is through these figures, Bakhtin continues, and especially through "the simpleminded incomprehension of the fool," that "a form was found to portray the mode of existence of a man who is in life, but not of it, life's perpetual spy and reflector; at last forms had been found to reflect private life and make it public."

Of course, to the author's long list of fleeting examples of such "reflecting" figures (from *Don Quixote* to the picaresque novels, from Le Sage to Marivaux, from Swift to Sterne), many more could be added. Much earlier, had not Socrates himself claimed to be an "idiòtes"? That is to say, a man lacking expertise, an ordinary man who was anything but knowledgeable? And what of Aristophanes who, in his caricature of him, not only lampoons his fogginess but does so in the context of the sublime lightness of *The Clouds*? This, not to speak of the "idiocy" of Christ, in whose name have spoken legions of men "possessed" – starting with the prophets. And surely the kingdom of heaven is not only a divine metaphor, but a mental one as well. One with an undeniably long life, thanks to Francis "the fool of God", the "idiot saints" among his followers and the likes of foolish moralists à *la* Sebastian Brant and Erasmus. Perhaps Prince Myshkin will have come to mind, the "altogether good man" who so totally obsessed Doestoyevsky as to compel him to write what is probably his masterpiece. And before then there'd been the mind-boggling reflections of *Les lettres persanes*, the ingenuousness of *Candide*, the fatalism of our good friend Jacques[2] and the long strain of eighteenth-century naturalism, with the likes of its *Paul et Virginie*. That's where Leopardi's errant shepherd[3] starts out (and what an error of precision that was!) and, to remain in the context of your tradition, there will follow Pascoli's "Little Child" and the airy and light-hearted Perelà, another figure with his head in the clouds, borne of the age-old imagination of the wily and naif Palazzeschi.[4]

All of the above seem to suggest that there exists a radical way not to be duped by the lies of appearances: not to understand them.

This is the road that the eccentric Kaspar has opened up within me, my dear Febbraro. And for all of your protests insisting on the authenticity, or originality, of the manuscript — I can already hear you rattling in your own defense! — I would like to be able to reply with a single, not ironic, but steadfast word: *literature.* If not for the fact, in all honesty, that the above-cited road or pathway, in spite of the very monuments that connect in my head and in the history of literatures, continues and leads else-where. Where, precisely, I cannot say. And it is as if this imprecision were to loom as one of its outcomes. At this point in time I can only speak of a resonance, of some-thing concrete that both touches and changes me; some-thing neither consoling nor irritating, in short — with all due respect for the century we've just left behind — neither avantgardistic nor restorational. But a heart, a place, forever conflicted. In Kaspar, yes, there is a strangeness; but it is a form of strangeness that fits, that I'd dare call productive. A strangeness *à la* Montaigne, which allowed that extraordinary man to fathom the truth in himself only by abolishing every systematic claim to Truth.

My doubts, you'll have gathered, are several. And along-side the rather obvious one, concerning the likelihood that behind Kaspar's misunderstandings lies the cozy lit-erary culture of his translator, there stands another which asks: who is the original and who the copy? Kaspar or you, my dear Febbraro? the misunderstood world of Kaspar or the other (idealistic) one of who lived by his side? And was the manuscript depicted in the *Requisite Preamble* con-cocted by you — that is to say, simply and purely created on the wings of a bizarre fantasy — or actually *found?*

Difficult words, you'll agree. Beware, however, of taking pride in them. Because even if you are but their "simple" translator, I take the liberty of reminding you that while we are surely responsible for whatever we find, only in small part are we deserving of it.

I do so hope to hear from you soon. And I would, of course, be delighted to welcome you again, whenever you wish. Until then, please receive my heartfelt greetings.

Yours,
Hernán Krantz

TRANSLATOR'S NOTES

1. All quotes from Bahktin's *The Dialogic Imagination* are taken from the translation by C. Emerson and M. Holquist (Austin: University of Texas Press, 1981).

2. The reference is to Diderot's *Jacques le fataliste et son maître*.

3. The reference is to Giacomo Leopardi (1798-1837) and his famous poem "Song of the Errant Shepherd".

4. The reference is to Aldo Palazzeschi (1885-1974) and his futurist novel *Il codice di Perelà*, in which the main character is a little man made of smoke, whose mysterious quality is at first celebrated and then condemned by society. See the English translation by N.J. Perella and R. Stefanini, *Man of Smoke*, Italica Press.

AUTHOR'S NOTE

Most of *The Diary of Kaspar Hauser* was written in the spring and summer months of 1995. The work is dedicated to Marco Rossetti, who many summers ago invited me to see a seminal film together, by Werner Herzog.

ANNUAL SPONSORS

EDITOR'S CIRCLE
Dr. Charles & Mary Rodning
Drs. Ron & Sue Walker
James & Megan Honea
Barry Marks, Esq.

SUSTAINING SPONSORS
Dr. Vivian Shipley
Nathan Blaesing
Harry & Rita Moritz
Dr. John Brugaletta

SUPPORTING SPONSORS
Steve & Dora Rubin
Eric and Kimberly Rubin
Kristina Marie Darling
Faith Garbin
Dr. Leonard Tenne

CONTRIBUTING SPONSORS
Nicole Amare
Dr. Betty Ruth Speir
Phyllis Feibelman
Harry & Dorothy Riddick
Gaylord Brewer

ABOUT SPONSORSHIP

Since 1981 Negative Capability Press has been committed to publishing quality books of exciting and innovative poetry, fiction, and nonfiction. We are a 501(c)(3) tax-exempt nonprofit organization and are designated by the State of Alabama as a Domestic Nonprofit Corporation. Our press is managed by a volunteer collective dedicated to independent publishing. Every dollar we earn is put directly back into our press—whether it is publishing our next book, marketing our authors, maintaining our website or increasing our distribution opportunities. It is you, our valued supporters, that will allow us to continue to publish beautiful, innovative books by amazing authors. We appreciate your support!

All sponsors will be acknowledged on our website and in our publications.

ANNUAL SPONSORSHIP LEVELS

Contributing Sponsor - $50—$99 per year
Supporting Sponsor - $100—$249 per year
Sustaining Sponsor - $250—$499 per year
Editor's Circle - $500 and up

Donations may be made at
www.negativecapabilitypress.org/donate
or by sending a check to:
Negative Capability Press, 62 Ridgelawn Dr. E,
Mobile, AL 36608